D0231953

MEN ON ICE

ANDREW GREIG

MEN ON ICE

Illustrated by James Hutcheson

CANONGATE

1977

SCOTTISH POETRY LIBRARY
Tweeddale Court 14 High Street
Edinburgh EH1 1TE
Tel: 031-557 2876

Publisher (Canongate)

MEN ON ICE first published in full by Canongate Publishing Ltd
17 Jeffrey Street, Edinburgh EH1 1DR, Scotland

© 1975, 1977 Andrew Greig

© Illustrations 1977 James Hutcheson

Parts of this work appeared in *Akros* no. 29, 1975

ISBN 0 903937 17 4 Hardback
     0 903937 18 2 Paperback

*Printed and bound in Great Britain by
Robert MacLehose and Co. Ltd
Printers to the University of Glasgow*

5615   C
(27.4.94)

MEN ON ICE

Being the story of 3 Climbers and . . . *another*

Dedicated to Dougal Haston, Climber.

PROLOGUE

on finding 'Men on Ice'

NO CAMERAS!

    Axe-man was adamant

Don't need no Real-to-Reel
   Recorder
to tell me I've been there,
I ken that fine.

        (There's some who every step
        must take a picture
        to prove to . . . who—
        themselves?
        they took it.)

We've heard enough
inanities from the Moon,

Aw Mi Gosh Whit A View!
—that's just a post-card
saying 'Wish You Were Here'. . .
when you're not.

I've got nothing to say
to anyone who
wants to know what
I've got to say
when I'm up there.

    —Buy second-hand experience,
    something gets lost in the wash.

Yon 'South West Face' boys,
only two interested me—
Haston wi' the pale blue eyes
who doesnae gie a damn
          for pictures

and auld MacInnes,
hauled off wi' snaw in his lungs,
'the fox of Glencoe'.

Ah but the Public
's got a right to know
    murmured Grimpeur
    condescending low
—if they can find us.

That's why
I've left my sketches and
Poet's notebook
waiting in the snow.

Let's see what they make of it.

'Wonderment and fear must be the prime ingredients. So the pilgrimage becomes an adventure.'

'The qualities that have given us domination over the beast, that demand safety not as a dead level of existence but in opposition to danger, continue to find an outlet in activities labelled dangerous, useless, or unjustifiable.'
—F. S. Smythe.

'In the mountains the shortest route is from peak to peak, but for that you must have long legs.'
—Nietzsche.

'. . . And the best fantasies rest on a sound notion of reality.'

'Thereafter sleep claimed its way and I moved
gently into another World of tangled dreams,
eased by a gentle flow of oxygen . . .'

—Dougal Haston, Everest S.W. Face, Camp 6.

INTRO

Let us define the terms of the game.
There are 3 men on the ice-face,
Grimpeur, Axe-Man, Poet.

They share the apprehension
of a fourth
estranged yet familiar
like the image in the mirror,

building the same world
the other way round
stretching out his left hand
to greet us
from the other side of the ice—

the *Zen Climber*
erstwhile 'The Bear'.

      Into the shifting spaces they inhabit
      let us drop a little time
      and join them
      in the Ice Fall

      A moment of crisis
      at high altitude
      20,000 feet
      and in the thin air
        their voices

            carry . . .

Captain Zen?

'But what is this to camel drivers smoking hashish?'

This is the truth of it:
bunched together on crumbling handholds
under a crazy overhang, the wind
screaming personal demons,
the snow outrageous, night setting in.
Worn down by a maze of dead endings,
baffling reversals, hopeful pitches
turned awry, the future terrifies,
it rears up beyond the vertical;
nor dare we look down
where the past glistens below
—a wicked diamond beauty—

Now each according to his nature
Marvels at his fate—

> Ma axe is USELESS against this
> wall of BLACK ICE! gasps Axe-man.

CORRECT Grimpeur observes,
Is this the END?

> Can it BE wonders Poet,
> Not even a WHIMPER?

> and he struggles with the urge
> that surges through the vein
> straight to his brain
> to lean back, let go,
> fall out with a final shout—
> luckily he can't stand pain.

I am G., let me
give my reading of this situation.
We three, touring through time
after our individual hearts' desire
seeking: splendour in action
> the final image of evening sun
> the golden thought,
are finally come to grief. It seems to be
a terminal case of entropy . . .

Poet
lost his typewriter
to Goat-Foot's satyrs—
no more Sky Writing.

Axe
abandoned his monkey-wrench in the Factory
a victim of the Metal Disease—
no more plumbing the Ocean Depths

I, Grimpeur
my thoughts are pale and dry
as the wind-bleached grasses of Winter
no more sinking in lush pastures . . .

—Don't give me that golden stuff,
Axe grunted
hammering in
his last piton,

Ah've had a great life.
On the ball
in the bed
wading in wi' ma axe.
Life is a gorgeous tit:
I wanted to feel it,
I felt it—
Phauggh! It was pulsating.
Now I've sucked it dry
and I'm ready to die.

I see   Poet sighing
as frostbite crept along
his finger bones,
my poems have been all wrong.
Instead of climbing the wall
they decorated it.
I never used one word
when two would do.

Shall I never sit down hereafter
to exercise this gift
and render this disaster

'. . . *erstwhile* "*The Bear*".'

into Poesie so subliminal swift
the Mood arrives ahead of its master Meaning,
as lightning does sullen thundering?

No one answered
and silence fell
between those loquacious pilgrims.

      Well, a man's gotta do
      what a man's gotta do
          as Herr Hitler said
          breathed Axe
          with sardonic leer.

      Pax, brothers. And he signed goodbye
      to life's parade
      as he prepared to leap—

      —But LOOK! The Zen Climber!
      Can he SAVE us?

          ah boys   you seem
          to be tied up here   chuckle
          Grimpeur pass me your HEMP ROPE

But Zen
   our situation is IMPOSSIBLE

          precisely   that's the first credible thing
          you've said all day   murmured The Bear
          cutting up Hemp Rope & stuffing it
          in pipe with hairy thumb   in this case
          the appropriate action is
                   Inaction
                   or
                   Action 'In'
          for you suffer from reality vertigo
          the view makes your head spin
                does it not
           here have a SMOKE
          and with a little aid you'll spot
          that crack on your left—

> *it opens into Plato's Cave*
> *there we may shelter*
> *in some safety undisturbed*
> *save for the passing*
> *of the odd philosopher . . .*

Mmm.

   Ahh.

Comfy!

> *Pass round the gentle persuader.*

This cave has remnants yet
   of myth & magick observed Poet
my eyes are drawn
      to glowing sketches on the walls
I see here the myth of Er
   and is that not Mithras
      at which Axe stares?

Huh,
messy, grumbled Grimpeur
it's cleaner in the
   'Philosophical Investigations'. . .

> *That may be so* remarked Zen
> *but Wittgenstein was a head of his time*
> *and his time is ahead of ours*
> *he passed this way often*
> *'alive with fiery breath'*

Pass the funny pipe
   mumbled Axe, never much one
   for this sort of conversation,
Last time I felt like this
   it was VE Day
and we'd drunk a bottle of pain-stripper
   in toast to peace eternal . . .

> *what—smashed again*
>   murmured Zen
>   crawling to his sleeping bag
> *very well*
> *let Poet tell a tale*
> *and then goodnight*
>   *my dizzy heroes*

6

Poet's Tale

Axe-man's hollow stare
was drawn straight to that portrait
of Bull and Bull-slayer
on the wall of our Cave-dwelling . . .
many a strange likeness flickered there
as I told An old tale in a new telling . . .

Well, at the appointed time
this Theseus shows up with a woman
        who is young, beautiful
        and in love with him
    and he is clean cut, respectful to his elders
    and very cool

the labyrinth he figures it out
with a little help from
what was her name

goes right in there
sword in one hand
in the other a rope

        he keeps going forward
            eyes blue & frozen
                till the heart of the matter
                    comes out at him

                    it was hot it was angry
                    it was the real thing
                    it was no man's brother
                    it was the great ding-a-ling

            till Theseus pushed his cool sword
            into that furious heart . . .
            icicle into a fire &
            the beast is at peace

                    and
                    the labyrinth is real quiet

                    just a little water
                    dripping

POET

                    the Hero can almost
                    hear himself . . .

                    think

                    (?)

            But he doesn't.

And so returns:

                    Senators wish to meet the exterminating angel
                    the Public touch his clothes
                    and buy their children
                    little swords and minotaur masks.

His steady ready lady
at the other end of the rope
has done her bit
    and he splits

                    then her island is real quiet
                    till warm Dionysos moves in
                        looking like an australian

                        (bronzed
                            boozed &
                                bollocking)

            —but she's just the lady of the tale.

They said it was
going to his head
and it was
            but not like that

    No, under that close-cropped hair
    was a banging and thumping and a black despair
    a din and a violence when people came round
    a madness that grew as he walked through the town

                        looking round
                        at all the people
                        looking so
                            ugly & down

9

he grew hot
he smoked gunpowder
his skin got itchy
he was a midnight prowler

and when he could disguise it
no longer
he left them

& prowled with his prow
with the emblem of bull
a maze of seas

roaring
roaring
roaring

like a MINOTAUR.

So Poet told his tale
as the last pipe went round. That night
we slept on air.

Cave Man

Stripped of Poet's sensual,
animate
and innately religious
wallpaper,
    the head interior
is a cool place to reside.

On the glass chair
   in the very centre of this room
   with 4 white walls
   folded in at the corners
   tilted like a Christmas hat
   on which he scribbles with blue pencil
   science's telephone numbers
   for long-distance connections with the Real
with folded hands
sits the mortician.

   Lest solipsism lead to fear
here is the corpse of a comforting thought;
let us cut it up
with some Witt:

      'We are not alone
        we are all one.
      For all our dis-parity
      (hypochondriac ghost of my social conscience)
      we are a Community of language-users
      for we play the same games
      and read the tribal newspaper over breakfast.

      What does this mean?

      This means we agree
      on the assignation of names
      to feelings that remain private
      on the basis of public display.

      This means?

      This means I know
      what you feel
      but I can never know
      how you feel it

GRIMPEUR

only you and God
(whom others might honour
for long life and leisure
to sink in cool thoughts
in this calm cave
my Cambridge college
so far below the mountain tops)
know that.'

I cannot tell you stories.
My analysis is offered as a cure
for insomania.

Some hours later.

O Sleep
why hast thou forsaken me
when even the Axe-man slumbers?

I could touch him awake, my brother,
across space he'd sympathise—
but no nearer; the 4th dimension
is that which lies
between one head and another.

Alone, I turn to fight the brain at midnight.

Existentially speaking
Grimpeur is a 'Cave' man
remarked Zen.
Does he not know this is a cul-de-sac?
Outside the wind still rages,
the light hawk is tethered to the air.

AXE

Axe-Man's Confession

I got this
       hot
in ma head
when people came round
they tangled together
like forests
whispering
    shutting out the good light,
    the good sound.

Once I walked
in the Town Library
in search of lightening
but it was I who bolted
from reading-room gloom
where shelves sag under weight of
dead wood.

       Ma mates swayed home
       arms round each other's shoulders
       thick-
              ets
       they rubbed guitars in long squeaks.

The family circle closed round me
Grow roots, or we'll choke ye.

       In time I tangled wi' the Copse
       for I,
              I was the good woodcutter
              with my bright axe
              I thinned the neighbourhood
              felled the old and rotten
              carved up the creepers
              pruned the young girls in their bloom—

It's good to see land cleared.
Quiet. I like that. I'm a
country boy at heart,
I told the jury.

When I grow up
I want to be a hunter.
I like to track the savage animals.
They look at me
with knowing eyes.

AXE-MAN IS INNOCENT!
Is he fuck.

Grimpeur & the Yobs

You want to know
why I don't like Axe-man, Poet?

When I was young
we had two pear trees;
both have since been cut down.
But at that time
yobs came from the town
under the fence like wolves.
We were meant to report them,
but I could never identify them;
they all looked the same
hair over their eyes
smelling of rotten food
and sour hunger
their eyes cunning
their words tricks
they killed frogs
with an air pistol.

One of them said I could
have a shot if I let him
at the pears
so I did
then he pointed the gun
at my head
and said
Right, ah'm gonna gie you a shott

I screamed I ran
they were forever aliens.

Now
look at Axe's eyes . . .

Zen on Poetry (1)

Poems themselves are not moving; it's
that a man should write them.

—Or, of course, a woman,—

—better still!—

18

Grimpeur's First Celestial Adventure

Friday afternoon. Down school corridors wondering
just when in childhood the golden
key out of the time-zone
had been mislaid
& now sought so feverishly . . .

    'Temperature rising & the
    juke-box blowing a fuse'
    pressed flat in this
    in many suddenly noticed ways
    too little town
    losing half my friends out of school
    and down on the turntable
    spinning when their number's jacked
    then rejected and neatly stacked
    outside the ministry of employ
    along the bars
    sinking jars
    talk talking of women & records & cars
    till their grooves wear thin . . .

    mad 17
    flute of bone
    carrying a rocket
    around in my pocket
    swearing in demonic french
    incense smeared mallarmé
    as my operating manual

    and mal armé I was until that afternoon
    until I took the capsule . . .

        SACREBLEU

    Sacred blue ! No key
but choirs & choirs
ripping sheets of space harmonies
across the slipstream of the blood
   now pounding on the ears
   as on an inner door

        —No door !

Deep in inner/outer space
free from the gravity of time
though always circling round it
the escape-hatch opens

dreamlike slow
the hero spread
eagled in the firmament
where either his head or space is bent

looking up and yawning
up into the awning

wanna i wanna
stay up here
where the day
never turns
into night

How long have i felt this sway

       Hey slam that door SHUT
       & come down at once boy!
       Are you out of your box?

that must be Janus Janitor
swimming silver-suited astronaut
into my field of vision

Take me to the HEAD
i said
Taken by the ear to the cool
       blue blue school pool
Janus crackling through the tight
helmet of his skull

       Allow me to illustrate
       a parable
       our being alive may be equated
       with our falling into water
       (throwing me in with a
       low trajectory)
       and our philosophy may be equated
       with what we do in there
       viz Strike Out In All Directions
       Life is not a game
       Games are something you may *choose* to play.

Pulled out (blue blue
shimmering on my blazer)
i am disarmed of my water pistol.

Take this stinking rag to the HEAD
muttered Janus to the Secretary as she
took down my particulars with a pencil

i took up my particulars with the merest blush
and dripping was shown into the study
(Quiet you angel voices).

Behind the desk sat the HEAD
His face was a study
i studied it
          Hm—eyes like wheels
            teeth like a trap
            the computer in heat

What's this,
Revelation?
Not in my school!   he snarled
Your tie is too gaudy
quit this childish
phosphoressence
you little twat.

              i took off my tie
              it was certainly a hallicimat
              (total dissociation within 2 seconds).
              There are no ties   i noted
              that is your collar troubling you
              no viewer need be troubled
              for there is no EYE.

NO I! gasped the HEAD
Why that's terrible!

i turned to depart—
No one may leave here without permission!
Very well well said i
call me creature of the stars
call me this nothing

'. . . the trail that somewhere in the mountain ends and tonight finds me campèd here with you, my Friends.'

you call me this astro nought
in your eyes i am no one
and this i may leave without your
scabby permission

What of Original Sinn
screamed the HEAD fortissimo
    and shivvered azure beading
    on my cuff

    Very well
    i wish to consult the blessed krishna

The Blessed WHO?   crackled the HEAD bursting
                   into white flames
                   glowing like the burning bush

  Wrong!
  The Blessed WHY
  There is no
  doctored who

Thus it came to pass
the HEAD blazed in the desert
of his parchment
& i left school for good
           good
               good
i was not consumed
        there is
        no
        consumption

And thus, concluded Grimpeur
kneeling at the last embers of our fire,
Did I first get higher
and take my first step on the trail
that somewhere in the mountains ends
and tonight finds me campèd here with you,
my Friends.

On Falling

No, Poet,
people are feared to fall *off*
and *out*

    off the ledge
    off the boil
    out of sight
    out of their minds

You be sure and fall *in*
and you'll take deep rest
in your deep-ression
when you fall as we all
do right down some terrible night
the spirit of gravity
locked round your shoulders
down through all the levels
into the ragged hole
in the heart
of the heart

then
when you can fall no further
when everything is permitted
but nothing is worth it

    walls fall away
    mountains are as glass
    wind plays violins
    on the other side of the ice

then the eye recoils from nothing
yet all things shine from within
you never know fear again

You call such men insane?
Their eyes are calm
surviving smoothly in a monstrous environment.

Grimpeur's Explanation

When I gathered from my backsliding
from my one-step-forward-two-back
progress through life

    that life was made of ice
    that life was perpendicular
    that the years are cruelly vertiginous

my will became ruthless
I went into my armoury
and started a design for
        Crampons

suitably shod
a man may climb the wall
even walk the ceiling
as Christ did except they called it
           water

there have been suggestions
that crampons, codeine & cocaine
are unethical aids
that our climb and our failure
must be done alone

O
but my powers
were made to be extended

& O
the high ice
is beautiful beyond belief

Inside an icicle I once saw
green grass preserved
and now the memory floods me

    I am in there
    on the other side of the ice

    I am a zen cow
    I munch miracles all day long

'. . . *an unknown yet certain destination*'

Praising the Woman

(Poet)

1

In the morning, blue-white
snow brightness;
at night car headlights,
on the ceiling, flicker.
We lie all day in bed, words
thickening with soft insistence
into the white afghan of sleep.
And when I wake in the darkness
we seem to be purring
towards an unknown, yet certain,
destination.

2

I sit up late by the fire,
wrist-wrestling with thoughts
that remained wordless
for you sleep now and I can
push this pen no further.
Still it snows, swirling
straight from the mountains
to come softing round her house,
a knock or a summons;
in the salt dark the shed door
swings and bangs in the wind.

I put away my books
and soon sleep washes out
the clouded mind, the milk bottle
swirled clean for tomorrow.
In the morning she will rake the peats;
they crumple to ashes with a faint sweet smell.

3
The only thing I know
about love: accept
no substitute.

The Oldest Game

Ah, the assent of women, sighed Poet,
Why don't you blunt your edge there, Axe-Man?
So Axe explained as night
slid over the ice.

Ma break came when I wis playing around
wi' the lads   we'd heard there was someone
looking fer talent   I made a few smairt moves
I've aye had style tae ma brut

so she signed me up
Put It There she said
so I did

And in time made her first eleven
an' made ma climb tae fame
putting it in from a' ways
in the heat of the moment nin faster

there wis animal roar
when I wis on the ba'
jist watching the replay
wud knacker ye

There wis some talk
o' long-term contract aye but
ye canna believe a'thing ye hear
in this game   lemme jist say

it's magick
when you're big
when you're Up There

Great till wan afternoon I went in
low and hard frae behind
aw I wis provoked ref
the wee black book for me

Frae then on I wis nowhere
tried too hard   lost the timing
running a' over the park
niver where the action wis

time I got there
it had moved on   I
couldna get tae the ba'

Na, the ba' game is fer mugs
tae mony folk after the wan thing
gimme the moonless nights
gimme ma axe

I play my ain game
agin the boys in navy blue
watch ma style

Reflections on the Mirror

(*Grimpeur*)

That is the haunting edge of glass;
the shadow of yourself
peering through it from the other side.

The light shifts and how
easily the shadow disappears;
the glass is clear
before the pane
the viewer stands alone again.

   World within mind
   Mind within world
   A shift of the light
   And the self is uncurled

Out in the mountains
the Mind problem is em-Bodied
in volcanic form:
if every peak is ideally projected
as on some inner silent screen,
what melancholy being is this travelling eye
that ants a way across the icescape?

I quiz Zen,
this mirror image glimpsed in glances,
this mote in the mountain corner of my I;
he flickers back into clear ice,
the prior source from which unfurled
the mystery of self and world.

     (If yon's a metaphysical theory of self,
     Me Physical Ta very much,
     grumbled Axe.
     Ah, never mind, Grimpeur,
     consoled The Bear,
     different foxes for different boxes.

Considering you used words
you stated the thought
in a ploughman's honest clumsy fashion,
holding the horses of the intellect
in an approximately straight line
across the crew-cut stubble fields that run
between the golf course and the ocean.)

Aye, very good, Zen.
You'll soon hae Poet
out o' a job—why not
stick to your rope-trick and the art
of maintaining motor cycles.

The Bear turned his massive head
and dissolved the Axe-man in his liquid eye.
Very well, he growled. *I like you,*
Stumpy, and your stubborn hand-Pict race.
For a mortal you're exceptional. Now
B. off—I must comfort our Poet.

Zen on Poetry (2)

So, Poet, your thoughts are quicksilver fish?
And the page the net to pull them in?
Very well: a fine haul
        they gasp and die
        in empty air

You can't eat them all at once
so quick!

            before they rot
            whip the guts out
            with a fishwife motion
            smoke them
            salt them in a barrel
            screw down the lid
            they make a tidy snack
            on winter nights when friends come round
            to do their heads in
            with home-brew

& fisher of words
    expect shrinkage

    the plump & shining thought
    when preserved

    is brown & shrivelled
    and quite quite

boneless

            The zen fisherman leaves
            his nets on board
            and lowers himself into the sea . . .

Hoof

Come, Axe, The Bear requested
as the last light rested
over the gloom of the Western Cwm,
Mak us Musik on yon silvery 'axe';
sweet music to unwind the mind
and hone the clouded judgement,
for today lies weary in the bone
and tomorrow is as yet unknown.

And so that physical man
with the head of the Hashshashin
complied, reached forth the hands of power
to play away the slack-tide hour
of aimless sorrow, that drifts
between the ebbing of today
and the rising of tomorrow;
his thread of melody sewed a seamless suture
between the present and our future.

Yet the healer as so often
was not healed
but all the while revealed himself
in the false fire of a memory flash
of a different land
where first his senses reeled
under the overtowering Rock Band . . .

'HOOF *emerges from his lair* . . .'

. . . T.A.M. drop out from the rain badweather violent hair en brosse
stomps through The Door to the music of a few 100 guitars
and SLAM turn those lights down   sweat crawling from
his toe-nails   but they can't! In the confused vegetable-
air scent and sweat slide across the leather skin of . . .
The Lizard holding down bassguitar forked tongue slitting
between his lips as he
leans back
on 500 Watt Stax
with his elongated 'axe'
booming up like concorde
(mania is his own reward)
and surveys with satisfaction
the action
below . . .
young Tam's eyes bulge as white strobes lobotomize
his lobes Turn Those Lights Off! slashing time & motion
into classic frieze of assassins & assassinated and my
god there's bull's horns on that HOOF that lead guitarist's
head & he roars as
                    200 weight of Middle C
shoot up the iron girders on the fat roof & the
Band Slam
into thundering boogie WILD THING . . .
rhythm-bass-drum 50 ton o' loco-motive running on
violent lines just WHAM WHAM and again WHAM remorse-
less inarticulate protest slamming heads back against the walls
imprisoned in 4/4 time till
we can stand this confinement no longer and HOOF
now
        Stepping Out
                        forward and Up
into immortal freedom
into a cage of white light a dog shameless
leather guitar swinging erect the lean
silhouette lifts endlessly as HOOF
emerges from his lair in white heat lets   'fly'
screaming volley of starshell notes
into the night of that sadistic SLAM, power cords
detonating down the spine:
concrete walls of prisoned sound now poised against

35

                                    the 'flight'
of this free agent extemporizing ex-tempo atonal
stone free from time and key hurtling through
space
notes cascading
clustery meteors showering Down
his white hands blur
like the saw wheel whir
and *he*
claws into *Metal*
Shreeking
and the crowd roar in ECSTASY !

          It is an emotion
that wears boots as Dionysos
lifts the roof in rapture
and the caretaker runs for the polis
& HOOF now pinned forever in young Axe's retina
learns the secret of Electric Guitar viz—
Infinite Sustain and now lets the long
long notes hang

             q^uive^r

                  toppl~e~

                       h ^a^ n ~g~

          in the raging ecstatic
cry of the white birds & soaring
out of the dream factory
one man's mind
swims in an ocean of bliss . . .

          Smoke
rising from the amps
          Sweat
dripping down the walls
truck loads of sound split wide open—The Lizard's
just playing Any Old Thing—spilling over
          weaving-sinuously bodies a
      shambles of messed fury
                    multi-coloured jackals
           pulling apart a wild guitar
                Screaming Mr Every pulls no weight

but searing to the back wall
scratches in hellish delirium for reason
      HOOF is building smokestacks through the smog
        as *flames* lick up the Stax
        and his axe
          EXPLODES
      & *freezes* him there on the Summit
             crackling with electricity
      & shattered head
        hazed in blue
          as his brains fuse
            you can hear him

   RAUGGH!

& young Theseus screams
for in the engine room things suddenly
  go wrong &
120 tons of fuzz
      sighing a tremendous groan
  burst through the Factory
& plug the frenzied half-wits in the corner
      where men and women
        are

          dis in teg ra ting . . . .

Yon bath o' ecstasy and death
all my violence drained
doon the plug 'ole,
clockwise.
All that remained
was tae tak tae mountains
secret as a mole,
fearin' to be human
hopin' to be whole . . .

   But Axe explained to them no more
   when to his ears came . . .
   unharmonious snore; swept
   in a rare moment of despair
   he wept while the others slept.

Morning in the Bhyundar Valley

Next Morning

'Morning in the Bhyundar Valley . . .
the mutations of the universe are apparent'

Good morning me!
thought Grimpeur
crawling from his sleeping bag,
Snakelike I slough off the skin
my night-self inhabited.
Ah sing us a song, Poet, a Lay
of the morning arising
over the mountains
of the preceding day.

O!

        (the Poet's cry leaped
         from his lips and ricocheted
         from peak to peak
         and each time echoed back
         more beaten out and bent
         till finally a shapeless sound
         like dew dispersed and, spent,
         sank into the ground . . .

That's all?

  How may I elaborate
  on Zero?

Huh?

      Sweet,
      sweet fuck all! laughed Axe,
      tuning up his 'axe'
      but for the benefit of this
      intellectual, this grimpeur
      who asks What Was That?
      even when he's been there,
      pray elaborate whiles I air
      ma G string
         and for our tenancy in this day, pay rent
         wi' music to delight the sense
         that wi' the heart experiments.

O : a cry of ejaculation
my cry of joy on this crystalline dawn
waking in fractured heads
as yet innocent of thought or desire
clear as the air up here

O the very picture of the self
the hoop of fire
unending stimulus
enclosing nothing
yet given shape by it
as is the rainbow by the air
it bridges

O the original sweet nothing

O is a portal
through which thoughts fly
and disappear

and no one know
where they go,

O!

Methinks Poet approaches his summit
quoth The Bear and left his cave
glowing and strong
like a morning sun emerging from dark mountains.

Grimpeur en Fer

'Il faut reculer pour mieux sauter!'—But how far?

I found Grimpeur in a parlous state.
Too smart for anything but words
he'd thought himself to a standstill
roped securely in
a lectureship
        camped 3 floors up
David Hume's Tower

& there he taught on 'possible worlds'
having no grasp
of this one

his face was blue
his hands too
he looked ready to vote
conservative—

      'Why, Gramps, you're half-asleep,
      you're about to Drop Off!'

        'Yeh,
        the nerveux climber's lost his nerve'
        sneered Axe.

Then Grimpeur turned and for the first
time I felt the
Heat of the man

      Look hollow eyes you
      vicious
      little
      sod

      what know you of *Nerves*
      who've got none
      who've never stood at the blazing cross
      roads of decision
      nor felt the pale two-fingered
      septic hand of scepticism
      tweak the very carpet from your
      cloven feet   and leave you
      sprinting the firmament!

41

SCOTTISH POETRY LIBRARY
Tweeddale Court 14 High Street
Edinburgh EH1 1TE
Tel: 031-557 2876

Hey Tam
your violent body's brave enough
and I'm afeared of it
but dropped into my *mind*
you'd soon be lost a-mazed
'alone & terrified'
and sobbing beat your
so-called brains out
on the midnight labyrinthian wall—

a season on fire
is more than
a systematic derangement
of the stomach
you
wouldn't last longer
than a snowbull in hell,
You'd be—FLASH-FRIED!

LOOK,

(as he threw off his ropes
leaned out over the abyss
and let it
wheel into him)

NO HANDS!

But—no words?
commented Zen
You dare?

And revelation grew in Grimpeur;
he fell on his knees and could
not speak

we carried him out
on the red hooves of sunset

silent

thoughtless

free

To Get Higher

(*Grimpeur*)

To get higher
how many lights
have burned out in the night
the brain at midnight overloading
glowing minds camped high
in the top flats of tenement buildings,
lives rising like rockets
trailing fire
to collapse insane on a street in Turin
arms round the neck of Dionysus.
What form of life is it
that uphauls itself
out of its element
to icy heights where the sun burns
and lungs heave
to thoughts unnatural and places inhospitable
to countless lives lost by accident or design?
Climbing into life
or out of it?

Back in the homelands
escapism is the charge,
fear the stimulus,
I the religion.
Escape from concentration camp
no blame says Zen.
See how they follow the hero's progress
with bated breath even as they sneer
and put their slippers on.
In the blue TV screen light
they yearn for our destruction
so they can put their shame to sleep
and yawning climb the stairs to bed
too little alive to ever be dead.

Outer space was our thrust . . .
the return was made
with a handful of dust.

43

So a generation came from West to East
to find the highest mountains
to conquer 'inner space'. . .
(if they could find it)
To Get Higher

Here we found koans
exits without entrances
monks chanting mantras
on a cherry-coloured morn
polite headshakes and immoveable silence.

They say we use . . .
too much force.
How else can ye climb? asked Axe
Whit kind o' heights are yon
where they don't even show us the mountain?

Let's say we found
guides and sherpas there
to hump our excess baggage . . .
servants who treat us as children.

   To Get Higher
so many fires quenched in the snow
eyes obliterated in dazzling madness
friends who disappear
without warning without explanation
on a solo attempt
when the weather turns bad.
And even those who have stood there
with 'the ultimate view'
on the height of personal Everest,
they Neverest. Only downhill thereafter
lucky to cash in the past
with a ghost
writer

in our colour supplements they appear
burnt out space heroes & mountaineers
Haston Aldrin Lennon Leary
'bearded and anxious'
'hiding behind a remote half-smile'.

I turn my wayward gaze
to the ground beneath my boot;
thinking not of peaks, I loot
them at every turning of the ways.
In here and now no step is up or down,
on in pain and hope and joy I go
until I love but do not linger on
each footstep in the snow.

'*the view   glaciers by night*'

Poet's Night Song &
Zen's Benediction

'The snow lies deep on glittering Soracte'

Meander meander
the river is tender
the heart too
tenderest when passing through

    immortals don't care

    they toss laughter like coins into the pool of our sorrow

    while over us light passes
    night passes
    we pass

Time takes all
as we wait for the death-fall
it's the domino effect
each moment topples the next
right up to Double Blank

    night without stars
    without friend
    without end

Death sits in
on every song or tale or smile
holding the last tile . . .

    Big Deal
    said Zen
    life's too short
    for a long face
    in the wrong place
    (a homily bee
    with a sting in the tale)
    You know it, Poet

    here, hang on to This
    (it's all that there is)

47

tonight we sleep on air
in the northern city
the view   glaciers by night
  love to you gentle listener
  now turn out the light

       sleep tight
       don't let the years bite

Aye, Pax
brithers. Cast honey sunsets
o'er the clouded scene, but pray
don't dull my eyes
wi' all your golden lull

—ah!—

—Bye!—

ZZZZZZZZZZZZZZZZZZZZZZZZZZZZZ
Z   Z
Z   Z
Z   Z
Z   Z
Z   Z
Z   Z
ZZZ^ZZZZZ

Grimpeur's Glossary and Index

Eyes, none, 21, knowing, 16, cunning, 17, Axe's hollow, 17, like wheels, 21, Dougal Haston's, vii

Fire, icicle into a, 7, trailing, 43, quenched in snow, 44, a season on, 42

Foxes, different boxes for, 30

G string, Axe-Man airs his, 39

God, 13

GRIMPEUR—mispron. 'Gram-Purr', from French ('Climber'). Born of a half remarkable question. The intellectual of the group. Good on thin ice and climbing in chilly, remote areas. Very technical. Nervous, highly-strung, talks to himself. A loner, owing to difficulty in conceding the existence of others. Fav. colour, White. Diversions: dialectic and drawing. His voice: *Legato*—smooth and connected (with traces of French accent).

Hashish, camel drivers smoking, 2

Haston, Dougal, Climber, Scot, v, vii, 49. Elements of Axe (physical courage and endurance) and Grimpeur (philosopher and introvert). *Hero.* (This collection and dedication predates his tragic death—*Ed.*)

Head, of his time, 6, gone to his, 9, interior, 11, not in ma, 15, gun at my, 17, bent, 20, of the hashshashin, 33, shattered, 37

Hitler, obligatory reference to, 5

Hoof—the paragorn of lead guitarists, brother to Axe-Man. Flight and death of, 35–7. See Minotaur.

Hume, David, his tower—academic pinnacle of Edinburgh University.

Ice, life made of, 25, other side of, 1, clear, 30, the high, 30

Ice Fall—broken glacier leading into Western Cwm.

Italics—usually indicates Zen's speech.

Jackals, multicoloured, 36

Janitor, Janus, 20

Lizard, The—Hoof's Bass Guitarist.

Mallarmé, incense smeared, 19

Minotaur, death of, 8, relation of Theseus to, 10. See also Bull, Hoof.

Nietzsche, collapse of, 43, quotes from, vi, 2, 24, 40

O, Poet's analysis of, 40. See also Zero, Sweet Fuck All.

Persuader, the gentle, 6

POET—born in a field, raised in a city. Love child. Possibly simple-minded, but gets there (has short-cuts). Secretary and cook to the Party. A useful link-man. Often called on to tell stories and set the scene. Took part in many early Epic Expeditions, but later concentrated on lightweight Lyrical assaults. Fav. colour, Sky Blue. Hobby, astronomy. His voice: *Con Brio*—with spirit; or possibly *Cantabile*.

SCOTTISH POETRY LIBRARY
Tweeddale Court 14 High Street
Edinburgh EH1 1TE
Tel: 031-557 2876